summertime food

m

summertime food

THE ESSENCE OF FRESH COOKING

written & photographed by

marc j. sievers

LITTLE PRINCE PRESS

HYANNIS PORT, MASSACHUSETTS
CHICAGO, ILLINOIS

Sievers, Marc J.
Summertime Food: The Essence of Fresh Cooking / Marc J. Sievers
Includes recipe index.
Cooking; Recipes

Library of Congress Cataloging-in-Publication Data is on file with the publisher.

ISBN-13: 978-1-7332885-3-8

LITTLE PRINCE
PRESS

Published in the United States by Little Prince Press, an imprint of
Marc-Ryan Group LLC
Hyannis Port Massachusetts USA 02647
Visit our website: littleprince.press
American made. Printed in the United States of America | 1

———— m ————

For all those sun-kissed summer memories, past and yet to come, where fresh cooking is at the heart of every great gathering.

Marc
xo

Introduction

"I hope these recipes help you create your own summer moments, your own traditions, your own memories of meals that taste like sunshine and feel like home."

—MJS

THE FIRST TIME I truly understood what summer was supposed to feel like, I was standing barefoot on the weathered deck of a Maine cottage, salt air drifting through the screen door as I watched my aunt effortlessly conjure a meal from whatever she'd found that morning at a farm stand just up the road. There were no complicated recipes, no stress about perfection—just ripe tomatoes still warm from the sun, sweet corn that had been picked hours earlier, and herbs she'd snipped from the window sill garden pots while her coffee was still brewing.

The whole meal came together in what felt like minutes, and we ate outside as the evening light stretched long across the yard, wine glasses sweating in the humidity, everyone talking and laughing over each other in that way that only happens when time slows down and the only place to be is in that moment—that glorious, loving, comfortable, delicious moment. That's what summer cooking should be—effortless, joyful, and completely focused on the moment you're in rather than the work it takes to get there.

I've spent decades chasing that feeling, and it's always right where I last left it here on the Cape, where summer isn't just a season but a way of being. It's the rush to get here and then time stretching out like hammock. It's in the tomatoes that actually taste like tomatoes, the corn so sweet you eat it raw while you're shucking it, buckets of sunflowers heralding the summer sun, berries that stain your fingers purple and the herbs that perfume your hands as you gather them. It's in the way a simple meal becomes a celebration when you move it outside, how a handful of the right ingredients can create something that feels both completely effortless and absolutely magical.

Summer has always been my season of possibility. The garden

cascades through its blooms, the days stretch endlessly, and suddenly there's time for all the things we promise ourselves we'll do when life slows down—impromptu dinner parties that spill into the yard, afternoon gatherings that turn into evening fêtes, meals that happen wherever the moment takes you. The kitchen becomes just one part of a larger stage that includes the garden, the porch, and even a beach blanket spread under the stars.

But here's what I've learned after years of summer entertaining: The magic isn't in complexity. It's in understanding that when ingredients are at their peak—when tomatoes burst with juice, when herbs release their oils at the slightest touch, when fruits are so perfectly ripe they practically cook themselves—your job isn't to improve them. Your job is to stay out of their way and let them shine.

The recipes in this book honor that philosophy. They're designed for busy summer days when you'd rather be outside than inside, for cooks who want to create something beautiful without missing the sunset, for anyone who believes that the best meals happen when you're not trying too hard. These are dishes that come together quickly but taste like you spent all day on them, meals that work just as well for a casual family dinner as they do for an elegant outdoor party. They are the essence of fresh cooking.

You'll find vibrant soups and salads that celebrate summertime, simple dishes that let the stove do most of the work, refreshing cocktails that taste like summer in a glass, and desserts that capture the essence of those long, lazy days you remember as a kid. Many of these recipes can be prepared ahead, assembled at the last minute, or served family-style so you can spend more time with your guests and less time running back and forth to the kitchen.

Because that's what summer cooking is really about—creating the

space for connection, for lingering conversations, for the kind of spontaneous joy that happens when good food brings people together. It's about remembering that the best entertaining doesn't require perfection; it requires presence. It's about understanding that when you start with ingredients that taste like the place and season they come from, you're already halfway to creating something unforgettable.

This book is my love letter to summer—to long days and warm nights, to meals that happen outside, to the particular magic that happens when fresh, simple ingredients meet good company and unbothered moments. I hope these recipes help you create your own summer moments, your own traditions, your own memories of meals that taste like sunshine and feel like home.

Now, let's head outside and revel in summertime food!

Ingredients Index

PANTRY STAPLES

These five basic ingredients are found in most recipes throughout this cookbook and should be pantry staples you always have on hand: **Black Pepper, Fleur de Sel, Olive Oil, Sea Salt, Unsalted Butter**

RECIPE INGREDIENTS

A

Apple (green Granny Smith) ... 47

Apricot-Lavender Preserves ... 33

Artichoke Hearts ... 39, 45

Arugula ... 25, 87, 95, 99, 121

B

Basil (fresh) ... 27, 37, 39, 41, 43, 45, 51, 59, 63, 71, 73, 75, 77, 79, 91, 95, 101, 105, 109, 111, 119, 121

Berry Medley (frozen) ... 61

Black Beans ... 115

Blackberries ... 29, 57, 135

Blue Cheese (Stilton) ... 99

Blueberries (freeze-dried) ... 125

Blueberries (fresh) ... 27, 129

Breadcrumbs ... 105, 115

Breadcrumbs (panko) ... 111, 121

Brown Sugar (dark) ... 133

Buttermilk ... 129

C

Cannellini Beans ... 113

Carrots ... 113

Celery ... 117

Celery Salt ... 67

Champagne ... 57, 63

Chardonnay (French wine) ... 111

Cheddar Cheese (English) ... 71, 105, 121

Cherry Tomatoes ... 37, 109, 119

Chickpeas ... 89, 119

Chili Sauce ... 67

Chives ... 31, 39, 49, 53, 71, 79, 83, 91, 93, 95, 101, 121

Chocolate (dark) ... 43

Cinnamon ... 29, 133

Coconut (unsweetened shredded) ... 29

Coconut Cream ... 135

Cognac ... 83

Cointreau (orange liqueur, triple sec) ... 57, 59, 63

Corn (Sweet Corn) ... 71, 77, 93, 115, 117, 121

Cornichon ... 83

Cream Cheese ... 39, 49, 129

Crème Fraîche ... 39, 129

Cucumber (English) ... 37, 73, 75, 101

Cumin ... 73

D

Dill (fresh) ... 49, 75, 79, 83, 117

Dijon Mustard ... 83, 93, 97, 99

Ingredients Index

Ingredients Index

Ingredients Index

Breakfast

EASY FRESH MORNING DISHES FULL OF FLAVOR

Eggs Provençal

THE ESSENCE OF SUN-KISSED SOUTHERN FRANCE

DIRECTIONS

① In a large bowl crack the eggs and whisk vigorously until the whites and yolks are completely incorporated and the mixture is a pale yellow. Set aside.

② In a large sauté pan set over medium heat, heat the olive oil. Once hot add onions and season with 1 teaspoon of salt and 2 teaspoons of cracked black pepper. Sauté for 7-9 minutes or until translucent and slightly tender. Next, add the garlic and sauté for another 1-2 minutes. Reduce the heat to medium-low. Add the butter to the center of the pan and melt.

③ Next, add the shredded mozzarella to the egg mixture, then add the rosemary, thyme, 1 teaspoon of salt, and 1 teaspoon of cracked black pepper. Whisk vigorously to thoroughly mix and immediately pour into the center of the sauté pan.

④ Gently stir the eggs, constantly scraping the bottom and sides of the pan with a spatula. The mixture will slowly come together and begin to thicken. Remove from the heat after about 8 minutes, when the eggs are wet-look-ing and gooey, but no longer runny. Continue to gently stir off the heat for another minute.

⑤ Next, transfer the eggs to the center of a serving platter. Top with fresh arugula. Drizzle a bit of olive oil over the leaves, and garnish with big shavings of parmesan cheese.

⑥ Serve immediately.

INGREDIENTS & PREP

Eggs – 12 extra-large, at room temperature

Yellow Onion – 1 medium, ¼-inch diced

Garlic – 6 cloves, finely minced

Rosemary – 2 tablespoons, fresh, finely minced

Thyme – 3 tablespoons, fresh, finely minced

Mozzarella – 1 cup, freshly shredded

Olive Oil – 3 tablespoons

Sea Salt – 2 teaspoons, divided

Black Pepper – 3 teaspoons, freshly cracked, divided

Arugula – 3 cups

Butter – 2 tablespoons, unsalted

Parmesan Cheese – For garnish, Parmigiano-Reggiano recommended

—

COOKING TIP

You cannot rush great eggs! They must cook on a medium-low heat; otherwise they will become tough and dry.

ANOTHER IDEA

You can also plate the eggs for each guest individually for a more formal feel. Divide the eggs between six plates and top each with ½ cup of arugula.

Triple Berry Oven Pancakes
WITH FRAMBOISE BUTTER

DIRECTIONS

FRAMBOISE BUTTER

1. In a small saucepan set over low heat, add the butter, framboise, and fleur de sel. Stir until the butter is melted. Set aside.

BATTER

2. Preheat the oven to 400 degrees F. Butter a half sheet pan (18in x 13in x 1in) with 1 tablespoon of butter. Line the bottom of the pan with a piece of parchment paper. Butter the top of the parchment paper. Lightly dust the entire pan with 1 tablespoon of flour. Set aside.

3. In a small saucepan set over low heat, melt the remaining 8 tablespoons of butter. Allow to cool slightly.

4. In a large bowl, add the milk, lemon juice, and lemon zest. Allow to sit for 10 minutes, until milk is slightly curdled. This process will mimic homemade buttermilk.

5. Next, whisk in the cooled and melted butter, remaining 2 cups of flour, honey, vanilla, vanilla bean paste, eggs, salt, baking soda, baking powder, and sugar. Whisk until just combined.

6. Using a spatula, fold in the berries. Transfer the batter to the prepared pan. Smooth the batter to cover the entire bottom of the pan.

7. Bake for 15-17 minutes, until lightly golden brown. Cut the pancake into 12 squares and serve with warm Framboise Butter.

INGREDIENTS & PREP

FRAMBOISE BUTTER

Butter – 8 tablespoons, unsalted, French recommended

Framboise – 4 tablespoons, Mathilde raspberry liqueur recommended

Fleur de Sel – ¼ teaspoon

BATTER

Butter – 9 tablespoons, unsalted, at room temperature, French-made recommended

Flour – 2 cups plus 1 tablespoon, all-purpose

Whole Milk – 2 cups, at room temperature

Lemon Juice – 2 tablespoons, freshly squeezed

Lemon Zest – 1 tablespoon, freshly zested

Honey – 3 tablespoons

Vanilla – 1 teaspoon, pure extract

Vanilla Bean Paste – 1 teaspoon

Eggs – 2 extra-large, at room temperature

Sea Salt – 1 teaspoon

Baking Soda – 1 teaspoon

Baking Powder – 2 teaspoons

Sugar – ¼ cup, granulated

Blueberries – ½ cup, fresh

Raspberries – ½ cup, fresh

Strawberries – ½ cup, hulled, ½-inch diced

Fresh Fruit & Yogurt Parfait

EASY, ELEGANT, DELICIOUS, AND SATISFYING

DIRECTIONS

① In a medium sauté pan set over medium heat, add the coconut and cook for 3-5 minutes until lightly toasted, tossing occasionally. Transfer to a dinner plate and set aside to cool.

② Next, in a large bowl, add the yogurt, vanilla, cinnamon, maple syrup, orange zest, and salt. Whisk until combined.

③ Lastly, evenly divide the yogurt into your desired serving vessels. Arrange the granola, blackberries, and raspberries over the top. Sprinkle with toasted coconut and garnish with fresh mint. Serve immediately.

INGREDIENTS & PREP

Unsweetened Shredded Coconut – ¼ cup

Greek Yogurt – 16 ounces, plain full fat

Vanilla – ½ teaspoon, pure extract

Cinnamon – ½ teaspoon

Maple Syrup – 3 tablespoons, Grade A

Orange Zest – 1 tablespoon, freshly zested

Fleur de Sel – ½ teaspoon

Granola – 1 cup, favorite store-bought brand

Blackberries – 1 cup

Raspberries – 1 cup

Mint – 4 sprigs, fresh, for serving

—

Serves 4

PREP TIP
You can prepare the yogurt up to 2 days in advance and store it in the mixing bowl, covered with plastic wrap, and set in the refrigerator.

NOTES

Lemon & Leek Frittata

INSPIRED BY FRESH INGREDIENTS AND BRIGHT FLAVORS

DIRECTIONS

1. Preheat the oven to 375 degrees F.

2. In a large bowl, add the eggs, half n half, chives, parsley, lemon zest, and Gruyère. Whisk until the yolks and whites are fully blended. Set aside.

3. In a 10-inch over-proof sauté pan set over medium heat, add the olive oil and butter. Once hot, add the leeks, salt, and pepper. Cook for 8-10 minutes until the leeks are tender, stirring occasionally.

4. Add the garlic and cook for just another 30 seconds, being careful not to burn the garlic.

5. Next, add the egg mixture. Stir to make sure all the ingredients in the pan are well distributed.

6. Continue cooking for 1-2 minutes, until the edges just start to set.

7. Transfer the pan to the oven and bake for 12-15 minutes, or until the edges are lightly browned and the center of the frittata is just set. (Be careful not to over bake the eggs or they will become tough and dry.)

8. Remove the pan from the oven and allow to rest for 5 minutes. The eggs will continue to cook as they rest.

9. Serve hot, warm, or at room temperature. Garnish with microgreens.

INGREDIENTS & PREP

Eggs – 8 extra-large, at room temperature

Half & Half – 2 tablespoons

Chives – 3 tablespoons, fresh, roughly chopped

Parsley – 4 tablespoons, fresh, roughly chopped, Italian flat-leaf variety recommended

Lemon Zest – 1 teaspoon, freshly zested

Gruyère Cheese – 1 cup, freshly grated

Olive Oil – 2 tablespoons

Butter – 2 tablespoons

Leeks – 2 medium-sized, washed, trimmed, ½-inch diced

Sea Salt – 1½ teaspoons

Black Pepper – 1 teaspoon, freshly cracked

Garlic – 2 cloves, finely minced

Microgreens – for serving

—

Serves 6

Very French Compound Butter

A LITTLE EXTRA LUXURY FOR LEISURELY MORNINGS

DIRECTIONS

① Place all the ingredients into a small bowl and mix until combined. Serve at room temperature.

INGREDIENTS & PREP

French Butter – 8 tablespoons, unsalted, at room temperature

Apricot-Lavender Preserves – 3 tablespoons, L'Épicurien brand recommended

Fleur de Sel – ¾ teaspoon

—

KITCHEN TIP

You can substitute any flavor of French preserves in the same quantity. If it contains large bits of the fruit then dice those pieces to help the butter blend more evenly.

IDEA

Try using this butter on croissants from your favorite bakery, on toasted country bread, scones, muffins—the possibilities are deliciously endless!

NOTES

_____
_____
_____
_____
_____
_____
_____

Appetizers & Cocktails

EARTHY AND ELEGANT BEGINNINGS TO ANY FÊTE

Summer Salsa

THE ESSENCE OF FARM STAND-FRESH IN A BOWL

DIRECTIONS

1. Add all the ingredients into a large bowl. Stir until well-mixed.

2. Serve with tortilla chips.

VARIATION
Try adding a can of drained and rinsed black or cannellini beans for extra body and flavor, served atop a bed of greens as a salad course.

INGREDIENTS & PREP

Lemon – 1 medium lemon, zested and juiced

Haas Avocado – 1 large, pitted, flesh removed, ½-inch diced

Strawberries – 8 ounces, hulled, ½-inch diced

English Cucumber – ½ large, seeded, ½-inch diced

Watermelon – 5 ounces, seedless, ½-inch diced

Cherry Tomatoes – 5 ounces, cut into quarters

Red Onion – 3 tablespoons, minced

Jalapeño – 1 large, fresh, seeded, finely minced

Basil – 3 tablespoons, fresh, roughly chopped

Mint – 2 tablespoons, fresh, roughly chopped

Olive Oil – 3 tablespoons

Sea Salt – 1½ teaspoons

Black Pepper – ½ teaspoon, freshly cracked

—

Makes 1 quart

PREP TIP
You can make this one day in advance and store in an air-tight container in the refrigerator.

NOTES

_____

_____

_____

_____

_____

_____

Leek & Artichoke Dip

AN ELEGANT AND CREAMY DIP SURE TO BE YOUR FAVORITE

DIRECTIONS

1. In a medium sauté pan set over medium heat, add the butter and olive oil. Once hot, add the artichokes, leeks, salt, and pepper. Cook for 7-10 minutes, until the leeks are tender, stirring occasionally.

2. Add the garlic and continue cooking for another 60 seconds, being careful not to burn the garlic.

3. Add the spinach and cook for another 2 minutes, stirring occasionally.

4. Stir in the crème fraîche, cream cheese, and Gruyère cheese. Heat until the cheeses are just melted.

5. Off the heat, add the basil, chives, peas, and the parmesan cheese. Stir to combine.

6. Serve with pita chips, tortilla chips, or your favorite crackers.

INGREDIENTS & PREP

Butter – 2 tablespoons, unsalted

Olive Oil – 3 tablespoons

Artichoke Hearts – 16 ounces, drained, roughly chopped

Leeks – 3 cups, white and light green parts, cleaned of all sand, ½-inch diced

Sea Salt – 1½ teaspoons

Black Pepper – 1½ teaspoons

Garlic – 3 cloves, minced

Frozen Spinach – 1 bag (16 ounces), thawed and squeezed dry

Crème Frâiche – 7½ ounces, at room temperature

Cream Cheese – 12 ounces, at room temperature

Gruyère Cheese – 1 cup, freshly shredded

Basil – ¾ cups, fresh, roughly chopped

Chives – 5 tablespoons, fresh, minced

Frozen Peas – 1½ cups, thawed

Parmesan Cheese – 1½ cups, freshly grated, Parmigiano-Reggiano recommended

—

Serves 6 to 8

SERVING TIP
You can serve this warm right from the pan, at room temperature, or even at the beach straight from the cooler!

NOTES

Provençal Tomato Jam
WITH HERBES DE PROVENCE

DIRECTIONS

① In a medium Dutch oven or heavy-bottomed pot set over medium heat, add all the prepared ingredients. Stir to combine. Bring to a boil, stirring often.

② Reduce the heat and simmer, stirring occasionally, for 55–60 minutes until the mixture has a consistency of thick jam.

③ Allow to cool, transfer into a jar, and store in the refrigerator.

INGREDIENTS & PREP

Tomatoes – 1½ pounds, cored, Roma, grape, or cherry varieties recommended

Herbes de Provence – 2 teaspoons, lightly crushed

Sugar – 1 cup, granulated

Shallot – 1 small, minced

Garlic – 3 cloves, minced

Lemon Juice – 1 medium, freshly juiced

Sea Salt – 1½ teaspoons

Black Pepper – 1 teaspoon, freshly cracked

—

Makes 1 pint

KITCHEN TIP
When choosing an herbes de Provence blend, make sure to choose one that includes lavender. This adds a delicate floral note to both sweet and savory recipes.

NOTES

_____

_____

_____

_____

_____

_____

_____

_____

Craquelins Savoureaux
SAVORY CRACKERS SWEETLY BALANCED

DIRECTIONS

1. Simply layer each cracker with a slice of Gruyère, a basil leaf, a dollop of honey (about the size of a nickel), and top with a piece of dark chocolate.

2. Arrange on a serving platter or flat board. Easily expand the recipe as needed.

A TASTY IDEA
Serve these Craquelins with a glass of port to finish a meal. An unexpected twist on dessert!

INGREDIENTS & PREP

Gruyère Cheese – 6 ounces, cut into 30 thin slices

Dark Chocolate – 3 ounces, roughly chopped

Basil – 30 small fresh leaves

Water Crackers – 30, plain

Honey – In a squeezable container

—

Serves 10

TIP
Meaning "savory crackers" in French, this quick and easy-to-assemble no-cook appetizer is perfect to bring to a party. Simply prepare all of the ingredients in advance, pack them all in to-go containers, and assemble at the party!

NOTES

_____

_____

_____

_____

_____

_____

_____

Marinated Artichoke Hearts

MEDITERRANEAN SUNSHINE IN EVERY TENDER BITE

DIRECTIONS

① Start by whisking together the garlic, oil, spices, lemon, and herbs in a medium-sized bowl.

② Add the artichokes to the mixture and toss well to coat evenly. Cover with plastic wrap and refrigerate overnight.

③ Serve at room temperature.

TIP
These Marinated Artichoke Hearts are perfect as part of a picnic. Pack them in Chinese take-out containers and bring disposable chopsticks. No cleanup!

INGREDIENTS & PREP

Artichoke Hearts – 1 jar (14 ounces), well drained

Olive Oil – ½ cup

Dill – 2 tablespoons, fresh, roughly chopped

Parsley – 3 tablespoons, fresh, roughly chopped

Basil – 2 tablespoons, fresh, roughly chopped

Lemon – 2 tablespoons, freshly squeezed

Lemon Zest – 2 tablespoons, freshly zested

Crushed Red Pepper Flakes – ¼ teaspoon

Sea Salt – ½ teaspoon

Black Pepper – ½ teaspoon, freshly cracked

Garlic – 3 cloves, finely minced

—

Serves 6

NOTES

Green Apple Guacamole

A BRIGHT AND TEXTURED UPDATE THAT IS CRAVE-WORTHY

DIRECTIONS

1. In a large bowl, add the freshly-squeezed lime juice and avocados.

2. Using two sharp knives in a crisscross action, slice through the avocados in the bowl until they are finely diced but still have some texture.

3. Lastly, add the remaining ingredients and gently toss.

INGREDIENTS & PREP

Lime Juice – 1 small lime, freshly squeezed

Hass Avocados – 3 ripe, pitted, flesh removed

Granny Smith Apple – 2 large, cored, ¼-inch diced

Jalapeño – 1 small, fresh, seeded, finely diced

Green Onion – ½ cup, thinly sliced, white and green parts

Parsley – ½ cup, finely minced, Italian flat leaf variety

Sea Salt – 1½ teaspoons

Black Pepper – 1 teaspoon, freshly cracked

—

Makes 3 cups

NOTES

Dill Pickle Dip

TANGY NOSTALGIA MEETS SOPHISTICATED SNACKING

DIRECTIONS

① In the bowl of a food processor fitted with a steel blade, add the garlic and all the pickles, reserving the juice. Pulse until coarsely chopped.

② Next, add the remaining ingredients and 3 tablespoons of the reserved pickle juice. Pulse until just combined. The dip should have a coarse texture.

③ Serve with potato chips, crackers, or alongside crudité.

INGREDIENTS & PREP

Garlic – 2 cloves, peeled

Baby Dill Pickles – 1 jar (16 ounces)

Cream Cheese – 8 ounces, at room temperature

Sour Cream – 8 ounces, at room temperature

Dill – 4 tablespoons, fresh, roughly chopped

Chives – 3 tablespoons, fresh, roughly chopped

Sea Salt – 1 teaspoon

Black Pepper – 1 teaspoon, freshly cracked

—

Serves 8

NOTES

Zucchini & Goat Cheese Rouleaux

ELEGANT BITES THAT SHOWCASE THE SUMMER SEASON

DIRECTIONS

1. Using a vegetable peeler, peel long thin strips going from end to end, discarding the first few strips as they will not be wide enough to fill.

2. Once you reach the seeds, rotate the zucchini, and do the same for the other three flat sides. Do this for the remaining zucchini.

3. Place the zucchini strips in a colander set over a bowl and sprinkle with 1 teaspoon of salt. Allow to sit for 30 minutes to draw out excess moisture, tossing occasionally. After 30 minutes, dry the strips on paper towels.

4. In a small bowl, add the goat cheese, remaining ½ teaspoon of salt, pistachios, 1½ teaspoons of oregano, pepper, and honey. Mix until combined. Transfer the mixture into a piping bag and snip off the end, making sure the hole is about ¼-inch in diameter.

5. Evenly pipe the mixture on the zucchini strips, then roll each strip and secure with a toothpick. Place the rolls onto a serving platter, drizzle evenly with olive oil, top each roll with a basil leaf, and serve.

INGREDIENTS & PREP

Zucchini – 3 medium, ends trimmed

Sea Salt – 1½ teaspoons, divided

Goat Cheese – 4 ounces, at room temperature

Pistachios – 3 tablespoons, finely chopped

Oregano – 2 teaspoons, dried, divided

Black Pepper – ½ teaspoon, freshly cracked

Honey – 2 teaspoons

Olive Oil – 3 tablespoons

Basil – ½ cup, fresh, whole leaves

—

Serves 6

Peach Cooler

AN EASY SUMMER SIPPER WITH A CHIC ZERO-PROOF OPTION

DIRECTIONS

1. In the jar of a blender, add the peaches and their juice, preserves, liqueur, and fleur de sel. Process on high for 15-30 seconds, or until well-blended.

2. Divide the puree into 6 glasses, top with sparkling water, garnish with fresh rosemary, and serve.

HIGH-OCTANE VERSION

To give this cooler a bit more zip you can substitute the sparkling water with chilled champagne, prosecco, or half the sparkling water with as much vodka or good-quality white rum.

ZERO-PROOF VERSION

To create a non-alcoholic version, substitute the peach liqueur with a natural peach syrup. Look for a 'sirop de pêche' produced in France as they are generally the most natural and often organic.

INGREDIENTS & PREP

Canned Peaches – 1 can (15 ounces)

Peach Preserves – 6 tablespoons

Peach Liqueur – 1 cup, Mathilde brand recommended

Fleur de Sel – ¼ teaspoon

Sparkling Water – 1 bottle (750ml), chilled, S.Pellegrino brand recommended

Rosemary Sprigs – 6, fresh, for serving

—

Serves 6

GARNISHING

Fresh rosemary, even as a garnish, adds a subtle herbaceous note. If you don't have rosemary, a simple leaf of fresh mint or basil will work in a pinch!

A LITTLE STORY

A few years back Ryan joined the ranks of non-drinkers to support his post-cancer health. But many times he was missing the pomp and pagentry of a cocktail, especially during those moments of cheers and glass clinking all around. His favorite stone fruit is peach and he loves rosemary, which are simply wonderful together. I created the zero-proof version of my Peach Cooler for him as an enjoyable alternative that he can sip and savor.

Jalapeño Lemon Drop Martini

CITRUS SOPHISTICATION WITH A BIT OF SUMMER HEAT

DIRECTIONS

1. Using the tip of a sharp paring knife, pierce the jalapeño pepper in 8-10 places. Cut it in half lengthwise, leaving the seeds and the ribs. Place the pepper in a 4-cup liquid measuring cup, pour in the vodka, cover with plastic wrap, and allow to sit at room temperature for 24-hours.

2. After 24-hours, discard the jalapeño and pour the tequila into a glass pitcher through a sieve to remove the seeds.

3. In a cocktail shaker filled with ice, add 3 ounces of the infused vodka, 2 ounces of lemon juice, 2 teaspoons of honey, and a small pinch of salt. Shake vigorously for 30 seconds.

4. Pour it into a martini glass, garnish with a thin slice of fresh jalapeño and lemon peel.

5. Repeat for the other 3 martinis.

INGREDIENTS & PREP

Jalapeño – 1 large, fresh

Vodka – 2 cups

Lemon Juice – 1 cup, freshly squeezed

Honey – 8 teaspoons

Sea Salt – ⅛ teaspoon

—

Serves 4

PREP TIP
You can make the jalapeño vodka in advance. After you infuse it for 24-hours and strain it, store it in an air-tight container (a canning jar works great!) for up to seven days in the refrigerator.

NOTES

_____

_____

_____

_____

_____

_____

_____

Fête Water

SPARKLINGLY REFRESHING FOR ENDLESS SUMMER GATHERINGS

DIRECTIONS

① Add the berries and mint leaves to a rocks glass and muddle to release the juice and essence of the mint.

② Next add ice, lime juice, triple sec, and champagne and gently stir.

③ Garnish with more fresh berries and mint. Serve.

AN IDEA

This refreshing and simple concoction of fresh berries, herbs, triple sec, and champagne is equal parts refreshing and chic. Even better is a recipe that can morph into something different depending on what you have on hand. You can change out the lime juice for fresh lemon juice, swap black berries and raspberries for strawberries, and use fresh basil instead of mint for an entirely new cocktail—just keep the measurements the same. Try other combinations as you like and keep track of them below.

INGREDIENTS & PREP

Raspberries – 2 whole berries, plus more for garnish

Blackberries – 2 whole berries, plus more for garnish

Mint – 5 leaves, fresh, plus more for garnish

Lime Juice – 1 ounce, freshly squeezed

Triple Sec – 2 ounces, Cointreau brand preferred

Champagne – 4 ounces, chilled

—

Makes 1 cocktail, expand as needed

ENTERTAINING TIP

Typically I avoid making individual cocktails when entertaining (I prefer to pre-batch them), but these are so simple to make and just take seconds—muddle, stir, pour, and sip!

NOTES

_____

_____

_____

_____

_____

_____

_____

Frozen Strawberry & Basil Margarita

A FLAVORFUL COOL-DOWN ON THOSE HOTTEST OF SUMMER DAYS

DIRECTIONS

① Add all the ingredients to the jar of a blender and process until smooth.

INGREDIENTS & PREP

Lime Juice – 1 ounce, freshly squeezed

Blanco Tequila – 2 ounces

Triple Sec – 1 ounce, Cointreau brand recommended

Strawberries – ½ cup, sliced, fresh or frozen

Ice – 1 cup

Basil – 6 medium leaves, fresh, plus more for garnish

—

Makes 1 cocktail, multiply as needed

VARIATION

Dress up the rims of ordinary glassware with dehydrated strawberries! Finely crush one cup of dehydrated strawberries and add them to a shallow plate. Add the juice of one lime to another plate. Next, dip the rim of a glass into the lime juice and then dip into the crushed dehydrated strawberries. You can do this one hour ahead of serving—just leave them at room temperature. This makes enough for six cocktails.

PREP TIP

Instead of freshly juicing limes while guests are anxiously awaiting cocktails, juice the limes ahead of time. Spoon the juice, in 1-ounce portions, into an ice cube tray and freeze them. Then just add perfectly portioned frozen fresh lime juice cubes into the blender.

NOTES

Rosé × Deux

BLUSHING PERFECTION FOR GOLDEN HOUR ENTERTAINING

DIRECTIONS

① In the jar of a blender, add the rosé, vodka, peaches, and berries. Process on low for 15-30 seconds, or until well-blended.

② Divide the cocktail mixture into 6 glasses, top with sparkling rosé, and serve.

INGREDIENTS & PREP

Rosé – 1 bottle (750ml), chilled

Vodka – ⅔ cup, chilled

Peaches – 1 cup, frozen

Berry Medley – 1 cup, frozen

Sparkling Rosé – 1 bottle (750ml), chilled

—

Serves 6

NOTES

It has twice the rosé, hence *deux* for two in French! Topping the finished cocktail with sparkling rosé before serving makes it feel like a soirée—bubbles simply make everything even better. Using frozen fruit not only keeps the cocktail cold, but also adds a bit of needed sweetness.

NOTES

_____

_____

_____

_____

_____

_____

_____

In The 6th Spritz

WHEREVER YOU ARE, PARIS IS ALWAYS A GOOD IDEA

DIRECTIONS

① Fill 6 large stemmed wine glasses with ice. Rub the rim of each glass with strips of grapefruit peel. Nestle the peels into each glass. Set aside.

② In a large pitcher, add the grapefruit juice, chilled rosé, and orange liqueur. Stir to combine.

③ Divide the cocktail evenly between the 6 glasses and top with a generous pour of chilled champagne.

INGREDIENTS & PREP

Grapefruit Peel – 6 strips, 2-inches long

Grapefruit Juice – 4 ounces, freshly squeezed

Rosé Wine – 1 bottle (750ml), chilled

Orange Liqueur – 4 ounces, Cointreau brand recommended

Champagne – 1 bottle (750ml), chilled

—

Serves 6

A LITTLE STORY

While testing and photographing my third cookbook *French Omelettes* in Paris I frequented Ralph's (Ralph Lauren's Parisian restaurant) and Café de Flore, both near to eachother on Boulevard Saint-Germain, and was inspired to create this cocktail capturing the essence of Saint-Germain-des-Prés in the 6th arrondissement of Paris.

NOTES

_____

_____

_____

_____

_____

_____

_____

_____

Citrus Garden Ice

LITTLE FROZEN JEWELS FOR SUMMER'S PRETTIEST DRINKS

DIRECTIONS

① Add all the juice and fleur de sel into a pitcher with a pour spout. Stir to dissolve the salt.

② Next, add a mint leaf to the well of each ice cube mold. Fill each well with juice and freeze for 8 hours, or overnight.

③ Store in the freezer for up to 1 month.

INGREDIENTS & PREP

Orange Juice – 1¼ cups (about 5 medium oranges), freshly squeezed

Pink Grapefruit Juice – 1¼ cups (about 2 medium grapefruits), freshly squeezed

Lemon Juice – ½ cup (about 3 medium lemons), freshly squeezed

Lime Juice – ½ cup (about 4 medium limes), freshly squeezed

Fleur de Sel – ¼ teaspoon

Mint Leaves – 30 small leaves

—

Makes 30 cubes (1-inch)

NOTE

Fleur de sel takes the bite away from the grapefruit juice and helps make the other citrus flavors come through with bright notes.

NOTES

_____

_____

_____

_____

_____

_____

_____

Sunday Morning Bloody Mary

TRANSFORM BREAKFAST INTO A LEISURELY SUNDAY BRUNCH

DIRECTIONS

1. Add all the ingredients (except vodka) to the bowl of a food processor fitted with a steel blade. Pulse 10-15 times until everything is well mixed.

2. Transfer to a large pitcher and chill for 1 hour.

3. Serve over ice for a zero-proof version, or add vodka to taste.

KITCHEN TIP

If you do not have a large-capacity food processor, you can easily process this in batches. You can also use a blender.

SERVING TIP

To create a generous experience, serve these Bloody Marys with stalks of fresh celery, and a skewer with cubes of a sharp cheddar cheese and a

INGREDIENTS & PREP

Prepared Horseradish – 5 tablespoons

Ketchup – ½ cup

Chili Sauce – 12 ounces

Sun-Dried Tomato Paste – 6 ounces

Tomato Paste – 12 ounces

Yellow Onion – 2 tablespoons, grated

Garlic – 3 cloves, finely minced

Lemon Juice – 4 tablespoons, freshly squeezed

Worcestershire Sauce – 2 teaspoons

Sriracha – 1 tablespoon

Celery Salt – 2½ teaspoons

Black Pepper – 2 teaspoons, freshly cracked

Water – 8 cups, cold

Vodka – to taste, your preferred brand

—

Serves 8

NOTES

_____

_____

_____

_____

_____

_____

_____

Soups & Sides

CHIC WARM-WEATHER SOUPS AND VIBRANT SIDES

Summer Corn Chowder

RICH AND CREAMY COMFORT—A STAPLE ALL SUMMER LONG

DIRECTIONS

1. In a large heavy-bottomed pot or Dutch oven set over medium heat, add the butter and olive oil. Once hot, add the onions, salt, and pepper. Cook for 10-12 minutes, until the onions are soft and translucent, stirring occasionally.

2. Add the corn kernels and garlic and continue cooking for another 5 minutes. Add the flour and turmeric and continue to cook for another 1 minute.

3. Next, add the potatoes, vegetable stock, and corn cobs. Cook uncovered for 15-20 minutes, until the potatoes are tender but not mushy, stirring occasionally.

4. Discard the cobs. Stir in the half & half and cheese and cook another 3 minutes.

5. Garnish with chives and serve hot.

INGREDIENTS & PREP

Butter – 8 tablespoons, unsalted

Olive Oil – ½ cup

Yellow Onion – 1 large, ¼-inch diced

Red Onion – 1 large, ¼-inch diced

Sea Salt – 2½ teaspoons

Black Pepper – 1½ teaspoons, freshly cracked

Sweet Corn – 7 large ears, kernels removed, reserve the cobs

Garlic – 5 cloves, minced

Flour – ⅓ cup, all purpose

Turmeric – 1 teaspoon

Yukon Gold Potatoes – 2 pounds, peeled, ½-inch diced

Vegetable Stock – 6½ cups, warm

Half & Half – 1½ cups, at room temperature

English Cheddar – ½ pound, freshly grated

Chives – fresh, for garnish

—

Serves 8

NOTE
Boiling the cobs extracts the milky liquid (corn milk) that's still in cobs. This milk is starchy, sweet, and adds extra flavor to chowder and will also help to thicken it.

Farm Stand Gazpacho

PEAK SUMMER IN A CHILLED, VIBRANT BOWL

DIRECTIONS

1. Add all the ingredients to a large bowl, reserving the tomato purée.

2. Next, using a food processor fitted with a steel blade and working in batches, process half of the mixture to a chunky consistency (think salsa). Process the other half of the mixture to be more liquid consistency (think tomato sauce).

3. As each batch is puréed, add it to another large bowl. Once all the ingredients are processed, stir in the tomato purée, making sure everything is well-mixed.

4. Cover and chill for 5 hours and serve cold.

SERVING TIP
Top each bowl of soup with a drizzle of olive oil and a few stems of microgreens. If you cannot find microgreens more fresh basil or even parsley can be fabulous.

ENTERTAINING TIP
You can make my Farm Stand Gazpacho up to three days ahead of time and store it in the refrigerator. The longer gazpacho sits, the more the flavor it develops. It is also a great no-spoil food option for the beach, packed in deli containers and stored in a cooler for those hot beach days!

INGREDIENTS & PREP

Roma Tomatoes – 3½ pounds, ripe, halved

Watermelon – 1 pound, seeded, rind removed, roughly copped

English Cucumbers – 2 large, peeled, seeded, roughly chopped

Green Peppers – 2 medium, seeded, roughly chopped

Red Onion – 1 medium, roughly chopped

Jalapeño – 1 medium, fresh, seeded, roughly chopped

Garlic – 3 cloves, minced

Basil – ½ cup, fresh, whole leaves

Parsley – ½ cup, whole leaves, Italian flat-leaf variety

Olive Oil – ½ cup

Red Wine Vinegar – ⅓ cup

Sea Salt – 1 tablespoon

Black Pepper – 1½ teaspoons, freshly cracked

Cumin – 1 teaspoon

Tomato Purée – 1½ cups

—

Serves 6 to 8

TIP
If you do not have a food processor, a blender, Vitamix, or even a stick blender will do the trick!

Chilled Cucumber & Mint Soup
COOL AND FRESH ELEGANCE

DIRECTIONS

① Add all the prepared ingredients to the bowl of a food processor fitted with a steel blade. Blend until smooth.

② Chill for at least 4 hours or overnight.

③ Serve with fresh slices of cucumber and a drizzle of olive oil.

INGREDIENTS & PREP

English Cucumbers – 2 large, peeled, seeded, roughly chopped (reserve a few slices for garnish)

Red Onion – ¼ small red onion, roughly chopped

Garlic – 3 cloves

Greek Yogurt – 16 ounces, plain full fat

Basil – 1 cup, fresh, whole leaves, lightly packed

Mint – ¼ cup, fresh, whole leaves, lightly packed

Dill – ½ cup, fresh, whole fronds, no stems, lightly packed

Olive Oil – ½ cup, plus more for garnish

Lemon Juice – 1 large lemon, freshly juiced

Sea Salt – 2 teaspoons

Black Pepper – 1 teaspoon, freshly cracked

—

Serves 6

NOTES

Brown Butter & Basil Corn

SWEET KERNELS DRESSED IN BUTTERY LUXURY

DIRECTIONS

1. In a 12-inch sauté pan set over medium-low heat, melt the butter and cook until it turns golden brown, or about 4-6 minutes, stirring occasionally.

2. Add the corn, salt, and pepper and sauté for 3-5 minutes, stirring frequently.

3. Remove from the heat, add the basil, and toss to combine.

4. Serve hot.

INGREDIENTS & PREP

Corn – 2 pounds, sweet corn kernels

Basil – 1 cup, fresh, roughly chopped

Butter – 8 tablespoons, unsalted, room temperature

Sea Salt – 1 tablespoon

Black Pepper – 2 teaspoons, freshly cracked

—

Serves 4 to 6

ANOTHER IDEA

If fresh corn is not in season, you can make Brown Butter Basil Corn with frozen corn. Defrost the corn in warm water for 5 minutes and dry thoroughly before adding to the pan.

NOTES

_____

_____

_____

_____

_____

_____

_____

Summer Herb Pesto

GARDEN ABUNDANCE CAPTURED IN EMERALD SPOONFULS

DIRECTIONS

1. In the bowl of a food processor fitted with a steel blade, add the pinenuts, salt, pepper, and garlic. Process for 30 seconds.

2. Add the basil, parsley, dill, mint, and chives. With the processor running, slowly pour the olive oil into the bowl through the feed tube and process until the pesto is thoroughly pureed. Add the lemon juice and Parmesan and puree for another minute.

3. Serve as a dip with crudité, over pasta, with grilled vegetables, or as a sauce with your favorite protein.

INGREDIENTS & PREP

Pine Nuts – ½ cup

Sea Salt – 1 teaspoon

Black Pepper – 1 teaspoon, freshly cracked

Garlic – 2 cloves

Basil – 2 cups, fresh, whole leaves, lightly packed

Parsley – 1 cup, fresh, whole Leaves, lightly packed, Italian flat-leaf variety

Dill – 1 cup, fresh, whole fronds, no stems, lightly packed

Mint – ½ cup, fresh, whole leaves, lightly packed

Chives – 1 cup, fresh, roughly chopped

Olive Oil – 1½ cups

Lemon Juice – 2 tablespoons

Parmesan Cheese – 1 cup, freshly ground, Parmigiano-Reggiano recommended

—

Serves 6

NOTES

Farmer's Market Pickles

THE SIMPLEST AND MOST FLAVORFUL DIY WORTH DOING

DIRECTIONS

1. In a medium saucepan set over medium heat, add the water and vinegar. Once it comes to just under the simmering point, remove the pan from the heat, add in the salt, and stir until it is dissolved. Allow the mixture to cool completely.

2. Fill any glass jar with a tight-fitting lid with your choice of cut vegetables like Kirby cucumbers or onions. Add fresh herbs, lemon zest, garlic cloves, whole peppercorns, crushed red pepper flakes—any flavor combination you love or want to try.

3. Fill the jar with brine, and seal the lid tightly. Place in the refrigerator for 5-7 days then enjoy!

INGREDIENTS & PREP

Water – 4½ cups

White Vinegar – 1 cup, you can also use apple cider vinegar

Sea Salt – 3 tablespoons

—

Makes 5½ cups of brine

A LITTLE STORY

I used to think making homemade pickles required lots of specialty equipment and a kitchen that spans the length of a city block. Well I was wrong, which doesn't happen often, just ask Ryan (or maybe don't!). Using just a saucepan, a few basic ingredients, and some jars with tight-fitting lids, I was able to make the most delicious and crisp Farmer's Market Pickles that truly bottle up the essence of summer! Use my recipe for the brine and have fun creating different combinations of flavors. And remember to make notes for yourself as you experiment!

NOTES

_____

_____

_____

_____

_____

_____

Classic Summer Condiments
UPGRADED FLAVORS FOR EFFORTLESS SUMMER FEASTING

INGREDIENTS & PREP

COGNAC KETCHUP

Ketchup – ½ cup

Tomato Paste – 2 tablespoons

Cognac – 2 tablespoons

Parmesan Cheese – 1½ tablespoons, freshly ground, Parmigiano-Reggiano recommended

Fleur de Sel – ¼ teaspoon

—

HERBED RELISH

Sweet Relish – ½ cup

Cornichon – 4 tablespoons, drained, minced

Dill – 4 tablespoons, fresh, minced

Chives – 2 tablespoons, fresh, minced

Fleur de Sel – ¼ teaspoon

—

THYME & LEMON MAYO

Mayonnaise – ½ cup

Thyme – 1 teaspoon, fresh, minced

Lemon Zest – 1 teaspoon, freshly zested

Lemon Juice – 1 tablespoon, freshly juiced

Fleur de Sel – ¼ teaspoon

Black Pepper – ¼ teaspoon, freshly cracked

—

FRENCHIE MUSTARD

Yellow Mustard – ½ cup

Dijon Mustard – 2 teaspoons

Whole Grain Mustard – 2 teaspoons

Honey – 3 tablespoons

Fleur de Sel – ¼ teaspoon

—

DIRECTIONS

① For each condiment, add the ingredients to a small bowl and stir thoroughly to combine.

NOTES

Salads

CELEBRATING SUMMER'S SUN-DRENCHED BOUNTY

Watermelon Salad & Citrus Vinaigrette

JUICY CUBES DRESSED IN CITRUS-ZESTY BRIGHTNESS

DIRECTIONS

CITRUS VINAIGRETTE

① Place all the ingredients into a jar with a tight-fitting lid. Shake vigorously for about 60 seconds until the vinaigrette is well-blended. Set aside.

WATERMELON SALAD & ASSEMBLY

② Add the watermelon and arugula to a large bowl. Drizzle with enough vinaigrette to coat the greens lightly and toss well.

③ Transfer the arugula and watermelon to a large serving platter. Drizzle over more vinaigrette, scatter over the microgreens, and top with parmesan cheese. Season with flaked sea salt and freshly cracked black pepper.

④ Serve immediately.

INGREDIENTS & PREP

FRESH CITRUS VINAIGRETTE

Olive Oil – ⅔ cup

Shallot – 3 tablespoons, very finely minced

Lime Zest – 2 teaspoons, freshly zested

Lime Juice – 2 tablespoons, freshly squeezed

Lemon Juice – 2 tablespoons, freshly squeezed

Orange Juice – 2 tablespoons, freshly squeezed

Sea Salt – 1 teaspoon

Black Pepper – ¾ teaspoon, freshly cracked

WATERMELON SALAD

Watermelon – 2½ pounds (measures 5 pounds with the rind), seedless, cut into 1-inch cubes

Arugula – 5 ounces

Microgreens – 2 ounces

Parmesan Cheese – ½ pound, large shavings using a vegetable peeler, Parmigiano-Reggiano recommended

Flaked Sea Salt – for serving

—

Serves 6

SERVING TIP
Try adding sliced avocado and black beans to make it into a main-course salad.

KITCHEN TIP
If you cannot find microgreens, reserve a handful of undressed arugula for the top to garnish and to add that pop of bright green. You can also use a handful of fresh mint leaves, flat-leaf parsley, and even basil leaves as a garnish.

Lime & Chickpea Salad

RICH, FULL-BODIED, AND BURSTING WITH FLAVOR

DIRECTIONS

1. In a large bowl, add all of the ingredients and stir until combine.

2. Allow to sit at room temperature for 30 minutes before serving.

INGREDIENTS & PREP

Chickpeas – 4 cans (15 ounces each), drained and rinsed

Lime Zest – 2 large

Mint – ½ cup, fresh, minced

Olive Oil – 6 tablespoons

Red Pepper Flakes – ½ teaspoon

Sea Salt – 1½ teaspoons

—

Serves 6

NOTES

A refreshing take on a classic chickpea salad. Lime and mint are a classic combination. This salad can be served cold or at room temperature. A great dish for a potluck or picnic. You can make it ahead of time and pack and go!

NOTES

_____

_____

_____

_____

_____

_____

_____

_____

Pesto, Pea & Arugula Pasta Salad

ALL THE FRESHEST ELEMENTS OF SUMMER IN ONE BOWL

DIRECTIONS

1. After the pasta has been cooked and drained, and while it is hot, place it into a large bowl.

2. Immediately add all the ingredients to the hot pasta and toss until evenly mixed.

3. Serve warm, at room temperature, or cold.

TIP

You can make this pasta salad in advance and store it in the refrigerator for up to three days. Before you serve it, taste test to see if it needs more salt, pepper, or even another handful of fresh arugula or basil mixed in.

INGREDIENTS & PREP

Fusilli – 1 pound, cooked al dente

Pesto – 7 ounces, store-bought

Grape Tomatoes – 2 pints, halved

Parmesan Cheese – 1 cup, Parmigiano-Reggiano recommended

Baby Arugula – 2 cups, washed and dried

Green Onions – ½ cup, thinly sliced

Basil – ⅓ cup, fresh, roughly chopped

Parsley - ⅓ cup, fresh, roughly chopped, Italian Flat-Leaf variety recommended

Red Pepper Flakes – ½ teaspoon

Lemon Zest – 1 small lemon, zested

Sea Salt – 1½ teaspoons

Black Pepper – 1 teaspoon, freshly cracked

—

Serves 4 to 6

NOTES

Sweet Corn & Lemon Pasta Salad

SUMMER'S GOLD TOSSED WITH CITRUS SUNSHINE

DIRECTIONS

LEMON VINAIGRETTE

1. Place all the ingredients into a jar with a tight-fitting lid. Shake vigorously for about 60 seconds until the vinaigrette is well-blended. Set aside.

PASTA AND SWEET CORN

2. Bring a large pot of salted water to a rolling boil. Add the dried pasta and cook according to package directions to al dente. During the last 3 minutes of cooking, add the sweet corn.

3. Drain well and transfer back into the same pot the pasta was coked in.

4. Add all the vinaigrette and stir until the pasta absorbs it all. Stir in the chives and parmesan cheese.

5. Transfer to a large serving bowl, season with more salt and pepper.

6. Serve immediately.

SERVING TIP
My Sweet Corn & Lemon Pasta Salad is equally delicious with the edition of halved cherry tomatoes and basil or diced avocado and parsley. Make it your own all summer long!

ENTERTAINING TIP
While you are at the farm stand picking up fresh sweet corn, grab a punch of sunflowers and some Italian flat-leaf parsley and create a fabulous arrangement. It's earthy, it's elegant, and it's the epitome of summer!

INGREDIENTS & PREP

LEMON VINAIGRETTE

Lemon Zest – 2 teaspoons, freshly zested

Lemon Juice – ½ cup, freshly squeezed

Honey – 4 teaspoons

Dijon Mustard – 1½ teaspoons

Olive Oil – ½ cup

Sea Salt – 1 teaspoon

Black Pepper – 1 teaspoon, freshly cracked

PASTA AND SWEET CORN

Medium Shells – 1 pound, dried

Sweet Corn – 5 medium ears (about 4 cups), kernels removed

Chives – ½ cup, fresh, cut into ½-inch lengths

Parmesan Cheese – 1 cup, freshly grated, Parmigiano-Reggiano recommended

—

Serves 6

KITCHEN TIP
This dish can be served hot or at room temperature. If you decide to serve it at room temperature, you might want to add a bit more lemon zest, salt, and pepper before serving to help brighten the salad as it sits.

Fresh Herbed Salad

A STROLL THROUGH THE GARDEN NEVER TASTED SO GOOD

DIRECTIONS

1. In a large bowl, add all of the greens and herbs. Toss together and arrange on a platter.

2. In a small bowl, add the salt, lemon juice, and olive oil. Whisk together and pour over the salad.

3. Serve immediately.

INGREDIENTS & PREP

Baby Arugula – 3 cups

Microgreens – ½ cup

Dill – ½ cup, fresh, whole fronds

Parsley – ½ cup, fresh, whole leaves, Italian flat-leaf variety

Tarragon – ½ cup, fresh, whole leaves

Basil – ½ cup, fresh, whole leaves

Chives – ½ cup, fresh, cut into 1-inch lengths

Fleur de Sel – 1 teaspoon

Lemon Juice – 4 tablespoons, freshly squeezed

Olive Oil – 4 tablespoons

—

Serves 6

NOTES

_____

_____

_____

_____

_____

_____

_____

On-the-Fly Lemon Vinaigrette

YOUR GO-TO SUMMER CITRUS DRIZZLE FOR NEARLY EVERYTHING

DIRECTIONS

① Place all the ingredients into a glass jar with a tight-fitting lid and shake vigorously for 60 seconds.

② Serve at room temperature.

INGREDIENTS & PREP

Olive Oil – ½ cup

Lemon Juice – 1 medium, freshly squeezed

Dijon Mustard – ½ teaspoon

Sea Salt – 1 teaspoon

Black Pepper – ½ teaspoon, freshly cracked

—

Makes ¾ cup

TIP
You can store this vinaigrette in the refrigerator for up to one week.

NOTES

Warm Pear & Mustard Salad

A SOPHISTICATED BLEND OF TEXTURES AND FLAVORS

DIRECTIONS

SALAD

1. Arrange the arugula, stilton and croutons onto a large platter. Set aside.

2. In a large sauté set over medium heat, add the olive oil and butter. Once hot, add the shallots. Cook for 3 minutes, stirring occasionally.

3. Next, add the pears, sea salt and pepper and continue cooking for 5-7 minutes, until the pears are tender.

4. Add the tarragon leaves and both mustards. Cook for 1 minute, stirring carefully to incorporate the mustards into the oil but to not break up the pears.

5. Lastly, spoon the entire mixture over the arugula, stilton and croutons, including all of the olive oil.

6. Give the salad a gentle toss, sprinkle with Fleur de Sel and serve warm.

BAGUETTE CROUTONS

7. In a medium sauté pan set over medium heat, add the butter. Once melted, add the bread cubes, salt, and pepper.

8. Toast for 3-4 minutes, tossing occasionally, until lightly brown.

9. Transfer to a bowl and set aside.

INGREDIENTS & PREP

SALAD

Baby Arugula – 3 cups

Stilton – 5 ounces, crumbled, at room temperature

Baguette Croutons – recipe below

Olive Oil – 6 tablespoons

Butter – 2 tablespoons, unsalted

Shallot – 1 medium, thinly sliced

Bosc Pears – 2 large, cored, 1-inch diced

Sea Salt – ½ teaspoon

Black Pepper – ¾ teaspoon, freshly cracked

Tarragon – 2 tablespoons, whole leaves

Dijon Mustard – 2 teaspoons

Whole Grain Mustard – 2 teaspoons

Fleur de Sel – for garnish

BAGUETTE CROUTONS

Baguette – 3 cups, cut into 1-inch cubes

Butter – 2 tablespoons, unsalted

Sea Salt – ¼ teaspoon

Black Pepper – ¼ teaspoon, freshly cracked

—

Serves 6

Grilled Peach & Mozzarella Salad
LIGHTLY CHARRED SWEETNESS MEETS CREAMY PERFECTION

DIRECTIONS

① Add the lime juice to a large bowl. Set aside.

② Place a grill pan over medium-high heat. When the pan is hot, brush the grill with a little bit of olive oil to make sure the peaches do not stick. Place the peaches, cut side down, on the pan and cook for 3-5 minutes, or until they are caramelized. Only cook the peaches on one side.

③ Remove the hot peaches from the pan, add them to the same bowl as the lime juice, and gently toss. Set aside.

④ Next, on a large serving platter add the greens, nestle in the sliced cucumbers, and scatter over the warm grilled peaches and torn mozzarella. Evely drizzle with olive oil then scatter over the basil leaves and chives. Sprinkle with fleur de sel and black pepper.

INGREDIENTS & PREP

Peaches – 3 medium, ripe, each cut into eight wedges

Spring Greens – 5 ounces

English Cucumber – 1 large, ¼-inch thick sliced

Bocconcini Mozzarella – 12 ounces, drained, torn into bite-sized pieces

Basil – 1 cup, fresh, whole leaves

Chives – ½ cup, fresh, minced

Olive Oil – ¾ cup

Fleur de Sel – 1½ teaspoons

Black Pepper – 1 teaspoon, freshly cracked

—

Serves 6

KITCHEN TIP
You can also grill the peaches on an outdoor grill. Place them away from the very hot center of the grill to make sure they do not overly char or burn.

SERVING TIP
Scatter over a can of drained and rinsed cannellini beans to make this a main course salad.

Family-Style

GENEROUS MAIN COURSES FOR SHARING ANY MEAL

Tomato & Goat Cheese Crostata

RUSTIC ELEGANCE WRAPPED IN GOLDEN PASTRY

DIRECTIONS

1. Preheat oven to 350 degrees F. Line a half sheet pan with parchment paper. Set aside.

2. In the bowl of a food processor fitted with a steel blade, add the flour, butter, sugar, white pepper, and ½-teaspoon salt. Pulse the food processor 10 times or until the butter is the size of small peas. Add the grated cheddar and pulse another 2 times.

3. Next, with the food processor running, slowly add the cold water down the feed tube, adding just enough for the dough to come together into a single mass. Turn the mixture out onto a floured surface and quickly shape into a ball. Cover the dough ball in plastic wrap and refrigerate for 30 minutes.

4. Once chilled, roll out the pastry dough onto a lightly-floured surface. Form into a 14-inch circle, ¼-inch thick. Transfer the disc to the prepared half sheet pan. Brush the pastry disc evenly with half of the egg wash and sprinkle with the breadcrumbs.

5. Arrange the sliced tomatoes on the pastry so they overlap, leaving a 2-inch border from the edge. Crumble on the goat cheese and sprinkle with 1 teaspoon of salt and the black pepper.

6. Next, turn the edge of the pastry in over the tomatoes, pleating the dough. The center of the Crostata will be exposed. Brush the remaining egg wash on the pleated pastry.

7. Bake for 40-45 minutes, or until golden brown. Remove from the oven, drizzle with olive oil, and garnish with basil leaves. Season with more salt and pepper to taste.

8. Serve either warm or at room temperature.

INGREDIENTS & PREP

Flour – 1½ cups, all-purpose

Butter – 8 tablespoons, unsalted, very cold, diced

Sugar – 2 teaspoons, granulated

White Pepper – ½ teaspoon, freshly cracked

Sea Salt – 1½ teaspoons, divided

English Cheddar – 3 tablespoons, freshly grated

Water – 8 tablespoons, very cold

Egg Wash – 1 extra large egg, lightly beaten with a splash of water

Breadcrumbs – 3 tablespoons, plain

Roma Tomatoes – 5 medium-sized, ¼-inch sliced

Goat Cheese – 3½ ounces, at room temperature

Black Pepper – 1 teaspoon

Olive Oil – 1 tablespoon

Basil – 10 small leaves, fresh, for garnish, fresh

—

Serves 6

Truffle Butter Fettuccine

INDULGENT SIMPLICITY FOR MEMORABLE GATHERINGS

DIRECTIONS

1. Choose your favorite fettuccine and cook following the maker's instructions.

2. Meanwhile, in a 12-inch sauté pan heat the olive oil over low heat. Add the garlic, red pepper flakes, salt, and black pepper. Sauté for 6 minutes until the garlic is tender but not brown. Turn off the heat.

3. Once the pasta is cooked to al dente reserve a ½-cup of the pasta water in a heat-proof measuring cup, then drain the pasta using a colander.

4. Immediately transfer the drained pasta into the sauté pan with the garlic. Add the butter and minced parsley and toss. If the pasta seems dry add a bit of the reserved pasta water as needed and toss.

5. Transfer to a large serving bowl and serve hot.

INGREDIENTS & PREP

Fettuccine – ¾ pound, cooked al dente

Crushed Red Pepper Flakes – ⅛ teaspoon

Kosher Salt – ¾ teaspoon

Black Pepper – 1 teaspoon, freshly cracked

Truffle Butter – 3 tablespoons

Olive Oil – 3 tablespoons

Parsley – 6 tablespoons, fresh, minced

Garlic – 5 cloves, minced

—

IDEA

This simple yet delicious pasta dish is perfect for a mid-week dinner or a Saturday night soirée! For a simple variation try tossing in 1 cup of grape tomatoes that have been cut in half lengthwise.

NOTES

Quinoa with Herbs & Tomatoes

WHOLESOME GRAINS KISSED BY GARDEN FRESHNESS

DIRECTIONS

1. In a 12-inch sauté pan set over medium heat, add the butter and olive oil. Once hot, add the red onion, sundried tomatoes, salt, and pepper. Cook for 5-7 minutes, until the onions are translucent.

2. Add the garlic and quinoa and cook for another 2 minutes.

3. Next, add the vegetable stock and tomato purée. Stir to combine. Reduce the heat to simmer, cover, and cook for 15 minutes, stirring once halfway through.

4. Remove from the heat and stir in the mascarpone cheese, cherry tomatoes, lemon zest, and parmesan cheese. Cover and allow to sit for 5 minutes.

5. Lastly, garnish with fresh basil, parsley, and a drizzle of olive oil. Serve hot.

INGREDIENTS & PREP

Butter – 2 tablespoons, unsalted

Olive Oil – 1 tablespoon

Red Onion – ½ small, ¼-inch diced

Sundried Tomatoes – ¼ cup, ¼-inch diced

Sea Salt – ¾ teaspoon

Black Pepper – ¾ teaspoon, freshly cracked

Garlic – 2 cloves, minced

Quinoa – 1 cup, uncooked

Vegetable Stock – 1 cup

Tomato Purée – 1½ cups

Mascarpone Cheese – 3 tablespoons

Cherry Tomatoes – 1 pint

Lemon Zest – ½ teaspoon, freshly zested

Parmesan Cheese – ½ cup, freshly grated, Parmigiano-Reggiano recommended

Basil – ½ cup, fresh, roughly chopped

Parsley – ½ cup, fresh, roughly chopped, Italian flat-leaf variety

—

Serves 6

TIP
Serve this right out of the pan at the table—no extra serving dishes required!

Hearts of Palm Gratins

TENDER AND LUXURIOUS BITES, A NOD TO COQUILLES SAINT-JACQUES

DIRECTIONS

1. Preheat the oven to 425 degrees F. Place 6 gratin dishes (7-inch diameter by 1½-inches deep) on 2 half sheet pans. Set aside.

2. In the bowl of a food processor fitted with a steel blade, add the butter, garlic, shallots, basil, parsley, lemon zest, salt, and pepper. Pulse until well combined.

3. Next, with the food processor running, slowly add the olive oil through the feed tub. Continue to run the food processor until the mixture is well mixed. Transfer the mixture to a medium bowl and stir in the panko. Set aside.

4. Add 1 tablespoon of chardonnay and 1 tablespoon of heavy cream into each gratin dish.

5. Evenly divide the hearts of palm rounds into each gratin dish. Top each one equally with the panko mixture.

6. Bake for 20 minutes, rotating the pans half way through, until the top is golden brown, and the wine and cream are bubbling.

7. Remove the gratins from the oven, top lightly with more fresh lemon zest and microgreens. Serve hot.

INGREDIENTS & PREP

Butter – 8 tablespoons, unsalted, at room temperature

Garlic – 2 cloves, peeled, roughly chopped

Shallot – ¼ cup, peeled, roughly chopped

Basil – 3 tablespoons, fresh, roughly chopped

Parsley – 3 tablespoons, fresh, roughly chopped, Italian flat-leaf variety

Lemon Zest – 1 teaspoon, freshly zested, plus more for garnish

Sea Salt – 1 teaspoon

Black Pepper – 1 teaspoon, freshly cracked

Olive Oil – 6 tablespoons

Panko Breadcrumbs – 1½ cups

French Chardonnay – 6 tablespoons

Heavy Cream – 6 tablespoons

Hearts of Palm – 4 cans (14 ounces each), drained, each stalk cut into 4 rounds

Microgreens – for garnish

—

Serves 6

SERVING TIP
Serve with the Watermelon Salad & Citrus Vinaigrette (page 87). The sweetness of the hearts of palm with the watermelon makes for a perfect (and very chic!) lunch or dinner.

Veggie & Quinoa Sliders
FRESH SIMPLICITY, INSPIRED BY THE CARLYLE

DIRECTIONS

1. Line a half sheet pan with parchment paper. Set aside.

2. In a medium saucepan set over medium heat add the quinoa, vegetable stock, ½-teaspoon of salt, and ½-teaspoon of pepper. Bring it to a boil, then cover and reduce the heat to a simmer. Cook for 15 minutes until all the liquid has been absorbed. Set aside.

3. As the quinoa is cooking, place a medium sauté pan set over medium heat. Add the olive oil. Once hot, add the red peppers, carrots, and onion, and remaining teaspoon of both salt and pepper. Cook for 8-10 minutes, until the vegetables are tender. Add the garlic and cook for 1 minute, being careful not to burn the garlic.

4. Transfer the vegetables to a large bowl and add the cooked quinoa, smashed beans, parsley, peas, and matzo meal. Stir to combine.

5. Using a 2¼-inch scoop, scoop the mixture into 12 balls by lightly rolling the mixture between the palms of your hands. Place each ball onto the prepared half sheet pan then gently press each into a patty, about ¾-inch thick.

INGREDIENTS & PREP

Quinoa – ½ cup, uncooked

Vegetable Stock – 1 cup

Sea Salt – 1½ teaspoons, divided

Black Pepper – 1½ teaspoons, freshly cracked, divided

Olive Oil – 4 tablespoons, plus more for frying

Red Pepper – 1 large, cored and seeded, ¼-inch diced

Carrots – 2 medium, peeled, ends trimmed, ¼-inch diced

Yellow Onion – ½ medium, ¼-inch diced

Garlic – 2 cloves, minced

Cannellini Beans – 1 can (15.5 ounces), rinsed, well-drained, mashed

Parsley – ½ cup, fresh, minced, Italian flat-leaf variety

Peas – ½ cup, frozen

Matzo Meal – ½ cup

—

Makes 12 sliders

6. In a medium sauté pan set over medium heat, add 2 tablespoons of olive oil. Once hot, add six patties to the pan and cook for 5-6 minutes on one side until golden brown. Then carefully flip each patty and continue cooking for another 3-4 minutes. Transfer the cooked patties back to the half sheet pan, wipe out the sauté pan, add more oil, and cook the remaining batch the exact same way.

7. Serve with slider buns, melted cheese, your favorite toppings, and potato chips!

Black Bean & Salsa Burgers

VEGGIE-POWERED PATTIES BURSTING WITH FLAVOR

DIRECTIONS

1. Preheat the oven to 375 degrees F.

2. In a single layer, add the drained beans to a half sheet pan. Roast for 8 minutes, toss, and continue roasting for another 5 minutes. Transfer the beans to a large bowl. Using the tines of a dinner fork, gently mash the beans—don't worry if they are not all perfectly mashed as some of the larger pieces will add texture to the finished burgers. Set aside. Line the same sheet pan with parchment paper and set aside.

3. In a medium sauté pan set over medium heat, add the olive oil. Once hot, add the red pepper, salt, and pepper. Cook for 5-7 minutes, until tender. Add the shallots, garlic, and corn and continue cooking for another 1-2 minutes.

4. Transfer the sautéed mixture to the same bowl as the beans and add the remaining ingredients. Stir until well-combined.

5. Using a 2¼-inch scoop, scoop the mixture and shape into 10 patties about 1-inch thick. Place the patties onto the prepared sheet pan and bake for 20 minutes, carefully flip each patty, and continue baking for another 10 minutes.

6. Serve hot on your favorite buns with a variety of toppings.

INGREDIENTS & PREP

Black Beans – 2 cans (15 ounces each), rinsed and well-drained

Olive Oil – 3 tablespoons

Red Pepper – 1 large, cored, seeded, ¼-inch diced

Sea Salt – ¾ teaspoon

Black Pepper – ¾ teaspoon, freshly cracked

Shallot – 1 large, minced

Garlic – 3 cloves, minced

Sweet Corn – ½ cup, fresh or frozen

Salsa – 1 cup, chunky variety

Hass Avocados – 1 ripe, pitted, flesh removed, mashed

Lime – 1 large, zested

Eggs – 2 extra-large, lightly beaten

Breadcrumbs – ⅔ cup, plain variety

—

Makes 10 to 12 individual burgers

TIP

This recipe makes 10 average-sized patties or 12 small ones (almost like a slider). You can even make them into mini sliders, just adjust the bake time!

Beach Shack Rolls

COASTAL COMFORT PILED HIGH

DIRECTIONS

1. In a medium sauté pan set over medium heat, add the butter. Once hot, add the corn, shallots, lemon zest, salt, and pepper. Cook for 2 minutes until the corn is crisp-tender. Remove from the heat and set aside to cool for 5 minutes.

2. In a large bowl, add the remaining ingredients and cooled corn and butter mixture, reserving the lemon wedges and dill fronds for garnish. Gently stir to combine.

3. Serve warm, at room temperature, or slightly chilled—all with lemon wedges and fresh dill fronds.

SERVING TIP
You can serve this in warm buttered and toasted hotdog, hamburger, or slider buns, as a side dish, or even as a salad on a bed of greens.

INGREDIENTS & PREP

Butter – 8 tablespoons, unsalted

Sweet Corn – 2 large ears, shucked, kernels removed

Shallots – 2 large, peeled, ¼-inch diced

Lemon Zest – 1½ teaspoons, freshly zested

Sea Salt – 1½ teaspoons

Black Pepper – 1½ teaspoons, freshly cracked

Hearts of Palm – 2 cans (14 ounces each), rinsed and drained, ¾-inch diced

Celery – 2 stalks, ends trimmed, ¼-inch diced

Green Onions – 2 stalks, ends trimmed, white and light green parts, thinly sliced

Dill – 2 tablespoons, fresh, finely minced, fresh

Parsley – 2 tablespoons, fresh, finely minced, Italian flat-leaf variety

Mayonnaise – ¼ cup

Old Bay Seasoning – ¾ teaspoon

Lemon Wedges – for serving (do not use the already-zested lemon)

Dill Fronds – for serving

—

Makes 1 quart

Quinoa Tabbouleh with White Beans
MEDITERRANEAN FRESHNESS AND WITH SATISFYING TEXTURE

DIRECTIONS

1. In a medium saucepan set over high heat, add 2 cups of water. Once it begins to boil, add the quinoa, salt, and pepper. Reduce the heat to simmer and cook for 15 minutes until the grains are tender. Drain, and transfer into a large bowl.

2. Add the remaining ingredients and mix to combine.

3. Transfer to a serving bowl and serve warm or at room temperature.

SERVING TIP

You can make this up to three days ahead of time. Once the salad has cooled completely, cover tightly, and refrigerate it. Remove the bowl from the refrigerator 45 minutes before you are ready to serve. Perk it right up with a big squeeze of fresh lemon juice and more salt and pepper.

INGREDIENTS & PREP

Tri-Colored Quinoa – 1 cup, uncooked

Sea Salt – 1 teaspoon

Black Pepper – ½ teaspoon, freshly cracked

Chickpeas – 1 can (15 ounces) drained and rinsed

Lemon Juice – ⅓ cup, freshly squeezed

Olive Oil – ⅓ cup

Green Onions – 5 stalks, ends trimmed, thinly sliced

Red Pepper – 1 large, seeded, ¼-inch diced

Parsley – 1 cup, fresh, minced, Italian flat-leaf variety

Basil – 1 cup, fresh, minced

Chery Tomatoes – 1 pint (12 ounces), cut in half through the stem

—

Serves 6

NOTES

Avocado & Sweet Corn Cakes

GOLDEN ROUNDS OF SUMMER'S BEST PARTNERSHIP

DIRECTIONS

① In a shallow dish, add the panko. Line a half sheet pan with parchment paper. Set aside.

② Next, in a large bowl add all of the ingredients, reserving the safflower oil and butter. Mix until well combined.

③ Using a 2¼-inch metal scoop (about 3 ounces), shape into 12 cakes. As you form each cake coat each side in panko. Place onto the parchment-lined half sheet pan. Cover with plastic wrap and refrigerate for 60 minutes or until firm.

④ Preheat the oven to 250 degrees F. Line a half sheet pan with two layers of paper towels. Set aside.

⑤ In a 10-inch sauté pan set over medium heat, add 2 tablespoons each of safflower oil and butter. Once hot, add 5 chilled cakes to the pan. Fry for 2-4 minutes on each side, until golden browned. Place the fried cakes onto the paper towel-lined half sheet pan and put into the warm oven. Repeat the same process, adding a bit more oil and butter, until all of the cakes are cooked, making sure to drain the second batch of cakes.

⑥ To assemble, in a large bowl, add the arugula and ¾ of the Lemon Vinaigrette. Toss to coat the leaves evenly, adding more as needed.

⑦ Divide the warm cakes onto six dinner plates, top with a handful of dressed arugula, shavings of Parmesan cheese, more salt and pepper and serve.

INGREDIENTS & PREP

Sweet Corn Kernels – 3 cups (about 4 ears)

Red Pepper – 1 large, cored, seeded, ¼-inch diced

Haas Avocado – 1 large, peeled, pitted, ¼-inch diced

Shallot – 1 large, ¼-inch diced

Chives – ¼ cup, fresh, finely minced

Basil – ¼ cup, fresh, finely minced

Eggs – 5 extra-large, at room temperature, lightly beaten

English Cheddar – 6 ounces, grated

Flour – 1½ cups, all purpose

Sea Salt – 1½ teaspoons

Black Pepper – 1 teaspoon, freshly cracked

Panko Breadcrumbs – 2 cups

Safflower Oil – for frying

Butter – unsalted, for frying

On-The-Fly Lemon Vinaigrette – page 97

Arugula – 5 ounces

Parmesan Cheese – 1 cup, large shavings, for serving, Parmigiano-Reggiano recommended

—

Serves 6

Dessert

ICONIC SUMMER SWEET TREATS

White Chocolate & Berry Krispie Squares

A CHILDHOOD FAVORITE BROUGHT TO AN ADULT LEVEL

DIRECTIONS

1. Line an 8-inch square baking pan with parchment paper. Set aside.

2. Next, in a large stockpot set over low heat, add the butter. Once melted, add the mini marshmallows, and heat until just melted, stirring constantly.

3. Remove the pan from the heat and add ½-teaspoon of fleur de sel and the remaining ingredients. Using a rubber spatula, stir until everything is well combined.

4. Transfer the mixture into the prepared baking pan and gently press into a single layer. Sprinkle the top with the remaining ½-teaspoon of fleur de sel.

5. Allow to set for 20 minutes, cut, and serve.

KITCHEN TIP
Use a tall stock pot when making these so you have plenty of elbow room to stir all the ingredients together and they stay in the pot rather than spill all over your counter!

INGREDIENTS & PREP

Butter – 6 tablespoons, salted

Mini Marshmallows – 10 ounces

Fleur de Sel – 1 teaspoon, divided

Rice Krispie Cereal – 8 cups

Freeze-Dried Strawberries – 1.2 ounces (about 2 cups)

Freeze-Dried Blueberries – 1.2 ounces (about 1 cup)

White Chocolate Chips – 11 ounces

Vanilla – 1½ teaspoons, pure extract

—

Makes 9 extra-large squares

SERVING TIP
You can easily cut these into 16 smaller squares to spread the deliciousness even further.

NOTES

_____

_____

_____

_____

_____

_____

_____

Triple Berry Flag Cake

THE STARS & STRIPES AS AN ICONIC SHOWSTOPPER DESSERT

DIRECTIONS

CAKE

1. Preheat the oven to 350 degrees F. Butter a half sheet pan. Line the bottom on the pan with a piece of parchment paper. Butter the top of the parchment paper. Lightly dust the entire pan with flour. Set aside.

2. In large bowl sift together the flour, salt, baking powder, and baking soda. Set aside.

3. In the bowl of an electric mixer fitted with a paddle attachment, cream together the butter and sugar on medium speed until light and fluffy.

4. Turn the mixer to low speed and add the vanilla, lemon juice, lemon zest, honey, and the eggs one at a time, allowing each to fully incorporate.

5. Next, add the flour mixture and buttermilk alternately, beginning and ending with the flour mixture.

6. Scrape down the sides and bottom of the mixing bowl. Gently fold in the berries.

7. Transfer the batter into the prepared pan. Tap the pan on a flat surface to release as many air bubbles as possible.

8. Bake for 35-45 minutes, or until a toothpick inserted in the middle of the cake comes out clean.

9. Remove the pan from the oven, allow the cake to cool in the pan for 10 minutes. Then, turn the cake out onto a wire rack to cool completely.

BUTTERCREAM & ASSEMBLY

1. In the bowl of a stand mixer fitted with a paddle attachment, add the cream cheese, crème fraîche, butter, salt, and vanilla. Turn the mixer to low speed and gradually add the confections sugar. Raise the speed to medium-low and mix until smooth.

2. Place the completely cooled cake onto a large serving platter or board.

3. Spread half of the icing on the top of the cooled sheet cake. Using a toothpick, outline the flag on the top of the cake. Fill the upper left third corner with blueberries.

CONTINUE TO NEXT PAGE →

DIRECTIONS

CONTINUED

④ Put the remaining buttercream in a pastry bag fitted with a large star tip and pipe two rows of white stripes. Place 2 rows of raspberries below the piped row to create a red stripe. Alternate rows of buttercream and raspberries until the flag is completed. Pipe small stars on top of the blueberries.

INGREDIENTS & PREP

CAKE

Flour – 3 cups, all-purpose, plus more for preparing the pan

Sea Salt – 1 teaspoon

Baking Powder – ½ teaspoon

Baking Soda – ½ teaspoon

Butter – 2 sticks, unsalted, at room temperature, plus more for preparing the pan

Sugar – 2 cups, granulated

Vanilla – 2 teaspoons, pure extract

Lemon – 2 large lemons, zested and juiced

Honey – ¼ cup

Eggs – 4 extra-large, at room temperature

Buttermilk – 1 cup, at room temperature

Blueberries – ½ pint, fresh

Strawberries – 1 pound, hulled, ¼-inch diced

—

MAKE AHEAD

The sheet cake can be made up to two days in advance. Once the cake has cooled completely, wrap it tightly in plastic wrap and store it in the refrigerator.

BUTTERCREAM

Cream Cheese – 1 pound, at room temperature

Crème Fraîche – 8 ounces, at room temperature

Butter – 1 pound, unsalted, at room temperature

Sea Salt – ¾ teaspoon

Vanilla – ½ teaspoon, pure extract

Confectioners Sugar – 1 pound, sifted

CAKE DECORATION

Blueberries – 1 pint

Raspberries – 1½ pints

—

SUMMER TIP

On a hot day you may have to periodically place the finished buttercream into the refrigerator for 5-10 minutes so it stays firm and easy to use while you decorate the cake.

Lemon Curd Ice Cream

SILKY TART SUNSHINE IN EVERY CREAMY SPOONFUL

DIRECTIONS

1. In a medium saucepan set over medium heat, add all of the ingredients. Whisk until the sugar is dissolved.

2. Transfer to a bowl and cover with plastic wrap pressing it directly onto the surface of the mixture. Chill the mixture in the refrigerator for at least 6 hours, or until very cold.

3. Once the mixture is chilled, add it to an ice cream maker and follow the manufacturer's directions.

4. Scoop out the ice cream into a freezer-proof container and freeze for 2 hours.

INGREDIENTS & PREP

Heavy Cream – 3 cups

Lemon Curd – 12 ounces, L'Epicurien brand recommended

Sugar – ⅓ cup, granulated

Fleur de Sel – ½ teaspoon

Honey – 1 tablespoon

Vanilla – 1½ teaspoons, pure extract

Limoncello – 4 tablespoons

Lemon Zest – 2 teaspoons, freshly zested

—

Makes 1½ quarts

ENTERTAINING TIP

You can scoop the ice cream into serving dishes a few hours in advance of serving and keep them in the freezer. Garnish with crushed cookies just before serving.

NOTES

Farm Stand Peach Ice Cream

SUMMER'S SWEETEST FRUIT CHURNED TO PERFECTION

DIRECTIONS

ICE CREAM BASE

1. In a medium sauce pan set over medium heat, add the heavy cream, sugar, honey, vanilla, and salt. Stir until the sugar is just dissolved, about 5 minutes. You can tell the sugar is dissolved by rubbing a bit of the cream between your fingertips, if there are no granulates it is done.

2. Transfer to a bowl and cover with plastic wrap pressing it directly onto the surface of the mixture. Chill until very cold, or overnight.

PEACH COMPOTE

3. In a medium sauce pan set over medium heat, add the butter. Once melted, add the peaches, dark brown sugar, and cinnamon.

4. Cook for 5-7 minutes, stirring occasionally, until the fruit is very tender and their natural juices start to release.

5. Transfer the mixture to a heat-proof bowl, cover with plastic wrap and refrigerate until cold, preferably overnight.

ASSEMBLY

6. Once the mixture is very cold, add it to an ice cream maker and follow manufacturer's directions. About 2 minutes before the ice cream base is finished churning, add in the chilled peach mixture and allow it to be fully incorporated into the ice cream base.

7. When ready, scoop out the ice cream into a freezer-proof container and freeze for 2 hours.

INGREDIENTS & PREP

ICE CREAM BASE

Heavy Cream – 3 cups

Sugar – ⅔ cups, granulated

Honey – 2 teaspoons

Vanilla – 1½ teaspoons, pure extract

Fleur de Sel – ½ teaspoon

PEACH COMPOTE

Butter – 2 tablespoons, unsalted

Peaches – 1 pound, skins on, pitted, ¼-inch diced

Dark Brown Sugar – ¼ cup, lightly packed

Cinnamon – ¼ teaspoon

—

Makes 1½ quarts

A LITTLE STORY

You guessed it, this is Ryan's favorite ice cream. A combination of perfect vanilla ice cream and peach pie, two of his favorite things. I created this recipe to combine the essence of his favorite summer treats.

Coconut & Lime Semifreddo

A TROPICAL ESCAPE IN FROZEN, CREAMY SLICES

DIRECTIONS

① In a medium saucepan set over medium heat, add the coconut cream, crushed lime leaves, honey, vanilla, sugar, and salt. Bring to a boil, then reduce the heat and simmer for 3 minutes, whisking occasionally.

② Transfer the mixture to a heat-proof bowl and cover with plastic wrap pressing it directly onto the surface of the mixture. Chill the mixture in the refrigerator for at least 2 hours, or until very cold.

③ Once the mixture is chilled, add it to an ice cream maker and follow manufacturer's directions. Line a one-pound loaf pan with plastic wrap and set it aside.

④ After the ice cream has churned, scoop the mixture into the prepared loaf pan, smooth out the top, cover, and place into the freezer for at least 2 hours, or overnight.

⑤ When you are ready to serve, add the berries and lime zest to a medium bowl and mash the berries with a dinner fork. Allow it to sit for 10 minutes.

⑥ Serve the semifreddo on a platter. To unmold, uncover the semifreddo and invert the platter over the loaf pan, then flip them over together and the semifreddo will unmold to be bottom-side up on the platter. Remove the plastic wrap. Slice into think pieces and top with the berries and their juices.

⑦ Serve immediately.

INGREDIENTS & PREP

Coconut Cream – 2 cans (13.5 ounces each)

Makrut Dried Lime Leaves – 6 leaves, veins removed, crushed

Honey – ¼ cup

Vanilla – 1½ teaspoons, pure extract

Sugar – ¾ cup, granulated

Sea Salt – ½ teaspoon

Raspberries – 6 ounces, room temperature

Black Berries – 6 ounces, room temperature

Lime Zest – ½ teaspoon, freshly zested

—

Serves 6

SERVING TIP

For even more flavor (and a boozy kick!), drizzle each serving with cold limoncello. The intense lemon flavor paired with the berries, lime, and coconut are a match made in flavor-heaven!

Recipe Index

"These are dishes that come together quickly but taste like you spent all day on them, meals that work just as well for a casual family dinner as they do for an elegant outdoor party. They are the essence of fresh cooking."

—MJS

Recipe Index

Recipe Index

Recipe Index

ALSO BY MARC J. SIEVERS

Entertaining with Love—*Inspired Recipes for Everyday Entertaining*

Table for Two—*Cooking & Entertaining for You and Your +1*

French Omelettes—*Your New House Meal*

Visit MarcSievers.com for more